This book belongs to:

_____

_____

Text by Patricia Keister
Designed by Patricia Keister
Edited by Trang.DT Design

Hello!

Coming from Maine, where it can snow for nearly half of the year, winter has always held a special place in my heart. As a child, days were filled with sledding and ice-skating and were always accompanied by rosy cheeks and mom's hot chocolate. It was a magical time of year. A snowstorm could bring with it such a beautiful peace and calm that blanketed the whole world as I knew it.

The weeks leading up to Christmas were a unique time of year. They were a time of preparing, a time of excitement, but also a time of quiet. The days were short and much of our day was spent in darkness. Yet, it was in this cold darkness that a warm light seemed to glow from within.

Living in Southern Vietnam we have two seasons— the rainy or dry season— and both are hot and sunny. There is no winter here. Keeping my family's traditions alive with my own daughters has always been important to me. I wrote this story to share with my daughters what winter and Christmas mean to me.

Patricia Keister

One chilly November morning, not so long ago,
Finn tomten was strolling through the forest.

He looked at the birch trees' pointy fingers scratching at the sky.

He listened to the soft whispering pines swaying in the wind.

He smelled the crisp air and smiled.
"Smells like snow," he said aloud.

The forest spoke to Finn and told him it was time to start preparing for Christmas. He cut some boughs from a fir tree and holding them up to his nose he closed his eyes. These would make a fragrant advent wreath for his table.

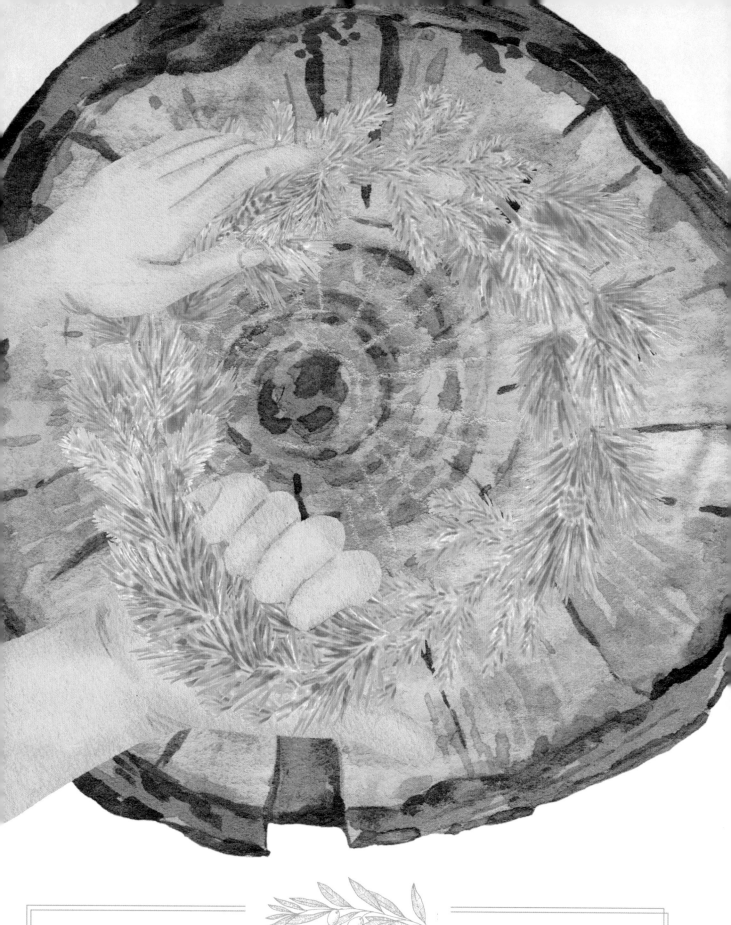

Once home, Finn went to work. His hands soon grew coarse as he pulled the branches into a tight circle.

Finn looked at his completed wreath. The fir boughs wrapped snugly around the four candles, holding them in place. These candles would guide him through the coming darkening days, a reminder of the light that soon would return to the forest.

The first of advent arrived. It had been snowy and cold but today the sun was shining. Finn went for a stroll in the forest admiring the glittering beauty surrounding him.

Tired from his walk, Finn found a rock with a rounded seat on which to sit and rest his feet. As he sat, the warmth from the midday sun flowed up from the rock and hugged his body.

Once home, as the sun was setting, he lit his first candle. The bright flame reminded Finn of the warmth provided him earlier in the day. He was thankful.

The second week of advent brought excitement as Christmas neared. Finn walked through the snowy forest searching for his Christmas tree.

He spied the perfect tree, but as he began his inspection his eye caught another tree not far away. Again and again, each time he found a tree he saw an even fuller tree just a bit further into the forest.

This journey for the perfect Christmas tree was joyous and fun. As he looked over each tree, he imagined it bringing Christmas to his home.

At last, he found just the right tree.

Back home, the tree's scent filled the air.
The green boughs brightened the dark corners
of the room. He lit his second candle.

As the third week of advent neared Finn began to dream of how his tree would look once decorated. He invited all of his animal friends to come and help him. Hedgie was fast asleep until Spring, but Squirrel and Hare would surely come to decorate the tree.

With his dearest animal friends all around, Finn placed his most prized ornaments on the tree.

His home glowed and warmed from the company of his friends. Finn lit the third candle on his wreath.

With preparations for Christmas nearly finished, a sense of calm began to settle as Finn felt a peacefulness all around him.

In the morning, Finn climbed a tall pine and looked out across the great world stretching below. Snow fell and the world was still.

At that moment he felt the peace that surrounded him warm its way deep into his heart. The connection he felt to all the world below brought a knowing smile to his rosy face.

Once home, Finn lit the fourth and final candle
on his wreath.

At last, Christmas had come.

Hi! I am Patricia, an early childhood educator and mom of two. I moved from the US to Vietnam over ten years ago to live and work. Wishing to share the seasonal living from my childhood with my own daughters, I started writing children's stories for them.

Making realistic-looking teaching materials for young learners both in the classroom and at home.

 teachingwithtricia@gmail.com

 @teachingwithtricia

Made in the USA
Monee, IL
02 December 2024

72190522R00019